My Dog

Siberian Husky

Priyanka Das

AV2

www.openlightbox.com

AV2

Step 1
Go to **www.openlightbox.com**

Step 2
Enter this unique code

AXPDKWE2I

Step 3
Explore your interactive eBook!

My Dog · AV2

Siberian Husky

Start!

⬆ Share

AV2 is optimized for use on any device

Your interactive eBook comes with...

 Audio
Listen to the entire book read aloud

  Videos
Watch informative video clips

  Weblinks
Gain additional information for research

Try This!
Complete activities and hands-on experiments

 Key Words
Study vocabulary, and complete a matching word activity

 Quizzes
Test your knowledge

 Slideshows
View images and captions

 Share
Share titles within your Learning Management System (LMS) or Library Circulation System

 Citation
Create bibliographical references following APA, CMOS, and MLA styles

This title is part of our AV2 digital subscription

1-Year K–2 Subscription
ISBN 978-1-7911-3310-8

Access hundreds of AV2 titles with our digital subscription.
Sign up for a FREE trial at **www.openlightbox.com/trial**

The digital components of this book are guaranteed to stay active for at least five years from the date of publication.

Siberian Husky

CONTENTS

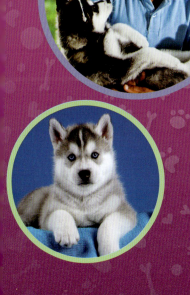

3

My Siberian husky is a smart and energetic dog.

He is friendly with people and other dogs.

Siberian huskies are medium in size. They look a little like wolves.

Dog Shoulder Heights

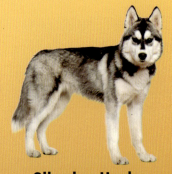

Australian Shepherd
Up to 23 inches
(58 centimeters)

Siberian Husky
Up to 23.5 inches
(60 cm)

Alaskan Malamute
Up to 25 inches
(64 cm)

My Siberian husky has a black and white coat. This is very common.

Most Siberian huskies have coats that are white and black, gray, or red.

Siberian husky puppies have bright blue eyes.

As they grow, their eyes may stay blue or change to brown.

Where in the World

Siberian huskies were bred by the Chukchi people in Siberia, which is part of **Russia**.

Siberian huskies are known for being sled dogs.

They can pull sleds over long distances in the snow.

My Siberian husky is very energetic.

We go for runs in the park.

14

He prefers cold weather
and often plays in the snow.

My Siberian husky has thick fur. It keeps him warm in winter.

I brush his coat often to keep it healthy and reduce shedding.

I feed my Siberian husky twice a day.

18

We spend time together. He also enjoys playing with other dogs.

19

I take my Siberian husky to the veterinarian at least once a year.

The veterinarian helps keep my dog healthy.

Dog Breed Popularity in the United States

#20

Shih Tzu

#21

Siberian Husky

#22

Bernese Mountain Dog

Incredible Siberian Huskies

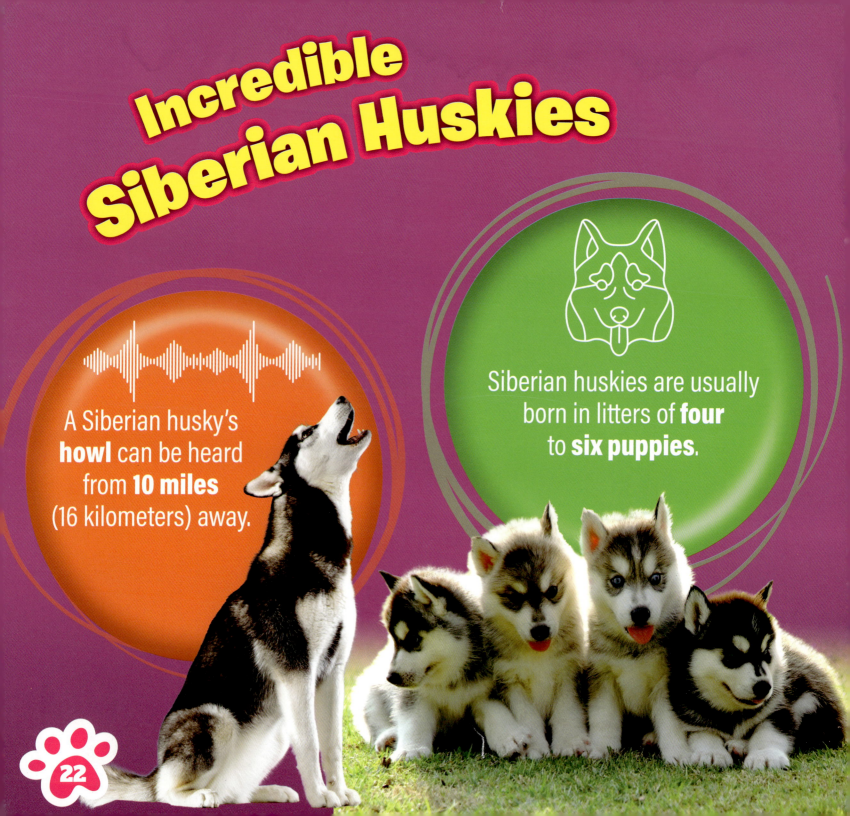

A Siberian husky's **howl** can be heard from **10 miles** (16 kilometers) away.

Siberian huskies are usually born in litters of **four** to **six puppies**.

Some Siberian huskies compete in sled dog races, such as the **1,100-mile** (1,770-km) **Iditarod race** in Alaska.

Siberian huskies can live in places as cold as **-75 degrees Fahrenheit** (-59 degrees Celsius).

23

KEY WORDS

Research has shown that as much as 65 percent of all written material published in English is made up of 300 words. These 300 words cannot be taught using pictures or learned by sounding them out. They must be recognized by sight. This book contains 63 common sight words to help young readers improve their reading fluency and comprehension. This book also teaches young readers several important content words, such as proper nouns. These words are paired with pictures to aid in learning and improve understanding.

Page	Sight Words First Appearance
4	a, and, he, is, my, other, people, with
6	are, in, like, little, look, they, to, up
9	has, have, most, or, that, this, very, white
10	eyes
11	as, by, change, grow, may, of, part, the, their, were, where, which, world
12	being, can, for, long, over
14	go, runs, we
15	often, plays
17	him, his, I, it, keeps
18	day
19	also, time, together
20	at, helps, once, states, take, year

Page	Content Words First Appearance
4	dog, Siberian husky
6	Alaskan malamute, Australian shepherd, centimeters, inches, shoulder heights, size, wolves
9	coat
10	puppies
11	Chukchi people, Russia, Siberia
12	distances, sled dogs, sleds, snow
14	park
15	weather
17	fur, shedding, winter
20	Bernese mountain dog, breed, popularity, shih tzu, United States, veterinarian

Published by Lightbox Learning Inc.
276 5th Avenue, Suite 704 #917
New York, NY 10001
Website: www.openlightbox.com

Library of Congress Control Number available upon request.

ISBN 979-8-8745-0426-7 (hardcover)
ISBN 979-8-8745-0427-4 (softcover)
ISBN 979-8-8745-0776-3 (static multi-user eBook)
ISBN 979-8-8745-0428-1 (interactive multi-user eBook)

032024
100923

Printed in Guangzhou, China
1 2 3 4 5 6 7 8 9 0 28 27 26 25 24

Project Coordinator: Priyanka Das
Designer: Jean Faye Rodriguez

Every reasonable effort has been made to trace ownership and to obtain permission to reprint copyright material. The publisher would be pleased to have any errors or omissions brought to its attention so that they may be corrected in subsequent printings.

The publisher acknowledges Getty Images and Shutterstock as its primary image suppliers for this title.